FIRE!

By Jeri Cipriano

Scott Foresman
is an imprint of

Glenview, Illinois • Boston, Massachusetts • Chandler, Arizona •
Upper Saddle River, New Jersey

Photographs

Every effort has been made to secure permission and provide appropriate credit for photographic material. The publisher deeply regrets any omission and pledges to correct errors called to its attention in subsequent editions.

Unless otherwise acknowledged, all photographs are the property of Pearson Education, Inc.

Photo locators denoted as follows: Top (T), Center (C), Bottom (B), Left (L), Right (R), Background (Bkgd)

Opener: ©Reuters/Corbis; 3 ©Reuters/Corbis; 4 (Inset) ©Michael S. Yamashita/Corbis; 6 (Bkgd) ©Michael S. Yamashita/Corbis; 7 (Bkgd) AP Images/©AP Photo; 8 (Inset) ©Jack Kurtz/The Image Works, Inc., (Bkgd) ©Jose Fuste Raga/Corbis; 9 (Inset) ©FRED GREAVES/©Reuters/Corbis; 10 (Bkgd) ©Michael S. Yamashita/Corbis; 11 (Inset) ©Deanne Shulman; 12 ©Ed Kashi/Corbis.

ISBN 13: 978-0-328-46919-2
ISBN 10:   0-328-46919-X

7 8 9 10 V010 13

   A wildfire is hot, smoky, and dangerous.
If the trees and brush are dry, a fire can
burn for days. If the wind is strong, a fire
can spread very quickly.

Some wildfires start far away from a road or a trail. Fire trucks and firefighters can't get to those fires. That's when they call in the smokejumpers.

There are about 400 smokejumpers in the United States. They go wherever there's a fire that's too big or too hard to get to.

Smokejumpers use a parachute to jump out of a plane over the fire. Their food, tools, and water are sent with another parachute.

Smokejumpers wear padded suits. The suit protects the person inside from heat, smoke, and flames.

Smokejumpers use very special tools to fight wildfires. One of these tools is called a *pulaski*. It has an axe on one edge and a hoe on the other. The hoe is used to cut into the ground.

Sometimes smokejumpers carry backpack pumps. But these can only be used if there is water nearby.

Smokejumpers get a fire under control so that the local firefighters can take over. Some fires take just a few days to control. But some fires are so bad that it could take a month!

In 1981 Deanne Shulman became the first female smokejumper. She was a smokejumper for 20 years. Today there are about 30 women smokejumpers.

Smokejumpers have a hot, dangerous job. Do they do it for the money? Here's one smokejumper's answer: "We get paid in sunsets!"